W9-ANW-393

Following Special Diets

by Beth Bence Reinke, MS, RD

BUMBA BOOKS™

LERNER PUBLICATIONS ◆ MINNEAPOLIS

Note to Educators:

Throughout this book, you'll find critical thinking questions. These can be used to engage young readers in thinking critically about the topic and in using the text and photos to do so.

Copyright © 2019 by Lerner Publishing Group, Inc.

All rights reserved. International copyright secured. No part of this book may be reproduced, stored in a retrieval system, or transmitted in any form or by any means—electronic, mechanical, photocopying, recording, or otherwise—without the prior written permission of Lerner Publishing Group, Inc., except for the inclusion of brief quotations in an acknowledged review.

Lerner Publications Company
A division of Lerner Publishing Group, Inc.
241 First Avenue North
Minneapolis, MN 55401 USA

For reading levels and more information, look up this title at www.lernerbooks.com.

Library of Congress Cataloging-in-Publication Data

Names: Reinke, Beth Bence, author.
Title: Following special diets / Beth Bence Reinke, MS, RD.
Description: Minneapolis : Lerner Publications, [2019] | Series: Bumba books. Nutrition matters | Audience: Age 4–7. |
    Audience: K to Grade 3. | Includes bibliographical references and index.
Identifiers: LCCN 2017048359 (print) | LCCN 2017047863 (ebook) | ISBN 9781541507739 (eb pdf) | ISBN 9781541503403 (lb :
    alk. paper) | ISBN 9781541526792 (pb : alk. paper)
Subjects: LCSH: Diet therapy—Popular works—Juvenile literature. | Diet—Juvenile literature.
Classification: LCC RM216 (print) | LCC RM216 .R3795 2019 (ebook) | DDC 615.8/54—dc23

LC record available at https://lccn.loc.gov/2017048359

Manufactured in the United States of America
1 – CG – 7/15/18

Table of
Contents

Special Diets

What you eat is called your diet.

Some kids follow special diets.

They do not eat certain foods.

Some people do not eat meat.

This is a vegetarian diet.

Kids with celiac disease
cannot eat wheat.
It makes them sick.

**Can you name
any foods made
with wheat?**

They can eat other grains.

Rice and corn are

usually safe.

Some kids have a food allergy.

They get sick or get a rash after eating some foods.

13

Some kids are allergic

to peanuts.

Others are allergic to milk.

What could kids with allergies do to keep from getting sick?

Kids with diabetes have

a special diet too.

Their bodies have trouble with sugar.

What kinds of foods have sugar in them?

They must limit sweets.

They must check how much

sugar is in their blood.

Kids on special diets eat

healthy meals.

But they stay away from

certain foods.

Do you follow a special diet?

Food Allergies

These are the eight most common food allergies.

peanuts

fish

wheat

shellfish

tree nuts

soy

milk

eggs

Picture Glossary

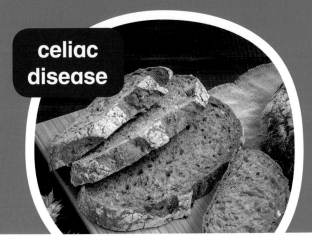

celiac disease

a condition that makes people sick if they eat a protein in wheat

diabetes

a condition where there is too much sugar in the blood

food allergy

a condition that makes people sick if they eat certain foods

vegetarian

a diet that does not include meat

Read More

Boothroyd, Jennifer. *Caution in the Kitchen! Germs, Allergies, and Other Health Concerns*. Minneapolis: Lerner Publications, 2016.

Clark, Rosalyn. *Why We Eat Healthy Foods*. Minneapolis: Lerner Publications, 2018.

McAneney, Caitlin. *Peanut and Other Food Allergies*. New York: PowerKids Press, 2015.

Index

Photo Credits

The images in this book are used with the permission of: © Monkey Business Images/Shutterstock.com, p. 5; © margouillatphotos/iStock.com, pp. 6, 23 (bottom right); © irina02/Shutterstock.com, pp. 8–9, 23 (top left); © BestPhotoStudio/Shutterstock.com, pp. 10–11; © ChesiireCat/iStock.com, p. 13; © SasaJo/iStock.com, pp. 14–15; © wavebreakmedia/Shutterstock.com, p. 17; © Fertnig/iStock.com, p. 18; © monkeybusinessimages/iStock.com, pp. 20–21; © Floortje/iStock.com, pp. 22 (top left), 23 (bottom left); © siamionau pavel/Shutterstock.com, p. 22 (top middle); © RusN/iStock.com, p. 22 (top right); © Lotus Images/Shutterstock.com, p. 22 (middle left); © nathanipha99/Shutterstock.com, p. 22 (middle right); © EasyBuy4u/iStock.com, p. 22 (bottom left); © oraya/Shutterstock.com, p. 22 (bottom middle); © domin_domin/iStock.com, p. 22 (bottom right); © Fernando Blanco Calzada/Shutterstock.com, p. 23 (top right).

Front Cover: © baibaz/Shutterstock.com.